Miniature Kites

Kites you can build that
actually fly while you walk

With 26 Plans

Second Edition

D1699774

Contents

- The fascination with miniature kites 5
- Sizes from giant to tiny 6
- Styles in miniature 6
- The small world of miniature kites 8
- Materials for building miniature kites 9
- Techniques for building miniature kites 10
  - Glue techniques 11
  - Tape techniques 12
  - Sail making 13
  - Framing your kite 15
  - Dihedral techniques 18
  - Bridle techniques 20
  - Tail techniques 22
  - Flying lines 23
  - General building tips 24
  - Flying your kite 25
- Plans for building easy mini kites 28
  - Peartop kite 29
  - Heart kite 31
  - Barn door kite 32
  - Guardian Kite 34
  - Comet kite 36
  - Butterfly kite 37
  - Mini Bird kite 40
  - Leaf kite 42
  - Sled kite 43
  - Penguin kite 45
  - Doodle kite 48
  - Chopstick kite 51
  - Noodle kite 52
  - Korean fighter kite 53
  - Rokkaku kite 54
  - Ghost kite 57
  - Train of kites 58
- Plans for moderate and challenging kites 61
  - Six friends kite 62
  - Single cell box kite 63
  - Genki kite 64
  - UFO kite 65
  - Roller kite 66
  - Firecracker kite 67
  - Hawk kite 68
  - Sparrow kite 69
  - Cody kite 73
  - Design your own kite 79
- Improving the flight of your kite 80
- List of websites 81
- Bibliography 81

About the author:

Glenn Davison is a designer, builder, and flier of miniature kites. He has won many awards for his miniature kite designs including, "best in flight," "most beautiful," and "smallest kite." Glenn's smallest kite to date is ¾" in its largest dimension. That's about the size of your fingernail. He intends to build a smaller kite in the future.

Don't miss these other kite books by Glenn Davison:

The fascination with miniature kites

Kites are a fascination and a passion for millions of people worldwide. The interest is universal across ages, cultures and throughout history. Miniature kites are a small part of that fascination. There's something magical about something as small and as delicate as a butterfly that can be built to fly gracefully on a string.

Miniature kites are delightful because they combine beauty, style, grace, playfulness, and fun into every small kite. There are a wide variety of styles, materials, colors, designs, and sizes from many countries worldwide.

Miniature kites can:
- fit in your pocket and transport easily
- be ready to fly at any time
- be made with little effort
- be used to prototype a larger kite
- easily demonstrate flight characteristics and kite styles
- be used to experiment with the dynamics of kite tails and bridles
- surprise people by flying and flying well
- be inexpensive
- look beautiful
- make great gifts
- make people smile

Here are the parts of a miniature kite. The spreader and spine are often called "spars:"

Sizes from giant to tiny

There are a multitude of kite sizes. Let's start with giant kites. They're huge, they're extreme, and they can be hundreds or thousands of square feet of lifting area. They can also be very expensive due to the cost of the fabric and the time to create them.

The kites that most people fly are in the range from 2' to 5' (60 cm to 1.5 meters.) This is an estimate of the length of the kite without a tail.

Small kites include many "kids kites" and fighter kites that are 12" to 24" (35 to 60 cm) tall.

But how small are miniature kites? They are typically 10" (25 cm) or smaller. That's about the size of your hand or smaller. They can be extremely small with the smallest being just a few millimeters tall.

Styles in miniature

If you look at the broad spectrum of kites there are *many* styles from *many* different countries. In general, "big kites" fall into categories such as:

- Flat kites
- Giant kites
- Delta kites
- Flexible kites
- Bowed kites
- Multi-line kites
- Cellular kites
- Soft kites
- Train kites and arch kites
- Traditional kites of paper and bamboo
- Miniature kites

The small world of miniature kites

Miniature kites maintain the diversity of their larger counterparts because the styles, designs, and colors of large kites are duplicated in a smaller size.

Multi-line kites are rarely seen in miniature, but you'll find single line kites in abundance.

Miniature kites are typically:
- Reproductions of historical kites
- Kites that fly at walking speed indoors
- Kid's kites that are simple and easy to build
- Ultra-tiny kites
- Ultra-lightweight kites
- Kites that fly outdoors

There are many kinds of miniature kites. You may see box kites, Cody kite variations, Rokkaku kites, kite arches, kite trains, fighter kites, character kites, antique kites, humorous kites, ultra-tiny kites, butterflies, bees, birds, bats, and many more.

You may see kites that represent different cultures such as Chinese art, Japanese art, Korean art, and a variety of kites from India.

Materials for building miniature kites

There are a wide variety of lightweight materials that can be used to build miniature kites. Some examples include tissue paper, plastic, napkins, hand-made paper, teabags, feathers, folded paper, and 200-year-old bamboo.

There are many choices for modern man-made materials such as nylon, polyester, mylar, and carbon fiber.

Many choices for kite-making materials can be found in your home right now, but remember, the most important factor in building small kites is the weight of the final product. If you're going to make a small kite, it must be very lightweight because, "lighter flies better."

Here are a few possibilities:

Spars	**Adhesives**	**Sails**	**Flying Lines**
Bamboo	White glue	Tissue paper	Nylon thread
Nylon fishing line	Yellow glue	Rice paper	Silk thread
Brush bristles	Model cement	Typing paper	Cotton thread
Balsa wood	Rubber cement	Wrapping tissue	Polyester thread
Glass fiber	Super glue	Polyester fabric	Rayon thread
Carbon fiber	Heat	Plastic bags	Human hair
Boron fiber	None	Films	Spectra

Tissue paper is available in a variety of colors and patterns.

Techniques for building miniature kites

On the following pages there are techniques you can use to build your own miniature kites.

You may prefer one technique over another. Unless you're building dozens of miniature kites the cost won't matter because the quantities are so small. But in certain situations, one technique may be:
- Easier
- Faster
- Lighter
- Stronger
- More precise
- More beautiful
- More adjustable (like an adjustable bridle instead of a fixed bridle.)

Whenever possible, choose the approach that results in the lightest kite.

Try different techniques and choose the methods you like best.

Glue techniques

The ideal glue or adhesive would form a perfect bond and have no weight. We can do even better than that by thinking of a bond that reduces weight and is stronger than the materials being joined. Interesting? Well, it's possible to form a terrific bond by melting two sheets of plastic together with a welding technique. You can use a soldering iron to tack two pieces together by melting holes. Doing that does reduce the weight!

Although melting isn't always practical, glue is very practical. Often, you will find that glue provides a stronger bond than the materials you're attaching together. Test it by gluing a seam between two pieces of paper. The result? The paper will tear but not at the seam.

Types of glue

There are many different types of adhesives available. These include white glue, yellow glue, glue sticks, model airplane dope, rubber cement, wood cement, plastic cement, CYA, contact cement, and silicone. The proper adhesive depends on the materials to be joined. Cement is recommended for joining wood to wood and model airplane dope is recommended for joining tissue to wood. Thinned water-soluble contact cement works well for gluing spars to Mylar. CYA is best for attaching nylon or polyester to carbon.

Glue application

Always use tiny amounts of glue:

Too much glue.   Less glue is better.

Most types of glue are perfectly fine for building miniature kites. Keep it light by using tiny amounts. Instead of pouring or smearing the glue, apply dots of glue with a toothpick. That helps to keep the weight down dramatically and helps it to dry faster.

Tip: Put one drop of glue into a bottle cap. It's mobile, it keeps your work area clean, and the bottle cap is disposable. Since you'd like to apply such tiny dots of glue, use a toothpick. One drop of glue is often enough to build an entire miniature kite. Sometimes the glue will dry before your work is done and you'll need a second drop!

Tape techniques

Tape is great for kite workshops because it's faster and cleaner than glue. Cellophane tape is very useful when building miniature kites because it is thin, lightweight and transparent. You can use tape to add strength, rigidity, and double-sided tape works well on plastics that are difficult to glue.

There are metallic Mylar tapes that come in many colors. Small pieces of these can be used for decorations.

Tip: Use tiny pieces of cellophane tape.
Tip: Avoid other types of tape that add weight.

Cutting tape

To attach tails or a bridle, you'll need tiny pieces of tape. Get a roll of 1/2" (12 mm) cellophane tape such as Scotch Magic Tape. It has a hazy color that is better than transparent tape which makes small pieces are difficult to see. Take a piece of tape, tape it onto the edge of your table and make a few small cuts as shown to create tiny strips. Cut off (or use tweezers to pull off) the strips one at a time. Make strips that are roughly 1/4" x 1/8". (6mm x 3mm) Prepare a few at the same time.

Three methods of taping the bridle:

Place the thread - then use tweezers to place a piece of tape over the thread and onto the kite at the same time.
Or…Combine the thread and tape - first, then use tweezers to place the "tape and thread" onto face of the kite.
Or… Use a needle - to pass the thread through the bridle point. Tape the thread onto the back of the kite.

Sail making

The shape and material of the kite sail are very important for steady flight so your kite sail should always be lightweight and symmetric.

Materials

Your kite sails can be made from gift tissue, wrapping tissue, rice paper, or washi paper. You can use a single layer of paper from a napkin, ripstop polyester, or plastic supermarket bags. You can also use food basket liners, bakery paper, taco wrappers, donut paper, and many other materials. It should be clean, unfolded, thin, and lightweight.

Tip: Some bakery papers have two different sides, a slick coated side and a matte side. When in doubt, glue to the matte side. The coated side may resist glue.

Weight

Use the lightest materials you can find. For sails, you can compare two different materials by dropping them from shoulder height to see which one falls more slowly. There are expensive scales that will measure as little as 0.1 grams, but you can build a balance cheaply by bending a piece of piano wire as shown then suspending your samples (of equal size) from the tips.

Arms of balance must be equal in length and weight

Symmetry

Symmetry means that the left side of your kite is equal to the right. They must be equal in area, angle, weight, and flexibility. This is very important for smooth, stable flight.

An easy way to maintain symmetry is by folding your sail in half then cut both sides at once using scissors, an X-Acto knife or a razor blade. By cutting both sides at the same time, both sides will have the same shape and area. You may want to use a ruler or a straight edge to keep your cuts straight.

Fold first

Then cut out pattern

Then unfold

Tip: You can cut two or more sails at the same time.

Tip: Use a template to cut your sails. If your template is made of paper, you can cut out the template while you cut out your first sail!

Decorating alternatives

There are many techniques for decorating your miniature kite sails:

Art paper	Some art papers are very interesting alone or in combination.
Inks, watercolors	You can also use inks, watercolors or pencil, but avoid heavy paints and crayons to keep it light.
Joining together	You can use tape or glue to join pieces of paper or plastic. This can be done with individual pieces, or in strips. Two pieces can be joined, or entire mosaics can be created.
Laser printing	Laser printing is possible by gluing or taping tissue paper to standard paper. Be *very* careful not to jam your printer.
Magic markers	Use magic markers to decorate your kite sails in many colors with very little added weight. Gel pens work well too.
Napkins	Napkins are pre-printed for every holiday and occasion and have two layers that can be carefully peeled apart.
Paper cuts	Paper cuts are one of China's most popular, historic, and characteristic folk arts. Paper cut kites are popular because of their beauty and detail. You can create your own by folding the sail in half, then use a razor knife or scissors to make small cuts in the sail to create a pattern, a picture, or a motif.
Plastic packaging	There are many pre-printed materials that are used in packaging food and toys. Be creative! Try using pre-printed plastic bags or product labels to make interesting and unexpected sails.
Rubber stamps	There are hundreds of rubber stamps in every size and shape. Rubber stamps are available for many pictures and logos.
Tracing	Most tissue paper is thin enough to use for tracing. Find your favorite picture, trace it onto tissue paper, then build the kite.

Tip: Decorate the sail while it's flat, before attaching frame, tails, or flying line. Prior to drawing, tape down the sail to prevent it from moving around.

Tip: Before using markers, test them on a scrap of sail material to see if the color bleeds.

Framing your kite

You can use many different materials to give your kite structure. Bamboo is very popular, but other options include paintbrush bristles, balsa wood, basswood, carbon fiber, fiberglass, straw from a broom, or strips of plastic from photo negatives or plastic from soda bottles.

There are times when you want your spars to flex. Thin bamboo, fishing line, and brush bristles are all good choices.

Stripping plastic

An easy way to create a lightweight frame is to find plastic, then use a ruler and a razor knife to cut strips. The same technique can be used with balsa wood, but not with bamboo.

Tip: Using plastic bottles means that the plastic is already curved.

Using bamboo

Bamboo has been used for making kites for more than a thousand years. It's strong, lightweight, and flexible. In some areas of the world it grows wild so it can be inexpensive or free.

Bamboo is a type of grass and there are hundreds of different kinds of bamboo. You can find it from many sources including Pier 1 Imports window shades, hobby shops, some back yards, and most supermarkets that provide bamboo skewers for grilling. Chopsticks are a poor choice because they're hard to split well. The bamboo should be dry before you split it.

Indoor frames vs. outdoor frames

Miniature kites that are built to fly indoors are lightweight and very delicate. If you're going to fly your kite outdoors, you should build a kite that has a stronger and more durable frame. The outdoor kite needs to handle a wider wind range, so a long tail is often required for stability in outdoor winds.

Tip: For miniature kites it's much easier to switch kites than to adjust a kite for wind conditions.

How to split bamboo

Do not cut bamboo. Carefully split it instead. It can be split into strips by pushing the knife through the entire length of the bamboo. See figure (a). Once it is split, you should take the best piece and split it again and again until the desired thickness is obtained. Bamboo can be shaved with a sharp knife, or sanded, to make the thickness even.

To check your finished spar, hold it between your fingers and flex it gently. If the thickness is consistent, it will flex evenly all around. See figure (b).

Attaching the frame

There are a few methods of attaching the frame to the kite:

- Glued to frame - The most popular method is to simply glue the frame directly to the sail. This is strong, permanent, and the glue adds strength even when the wood is extremely thin.

Other methods include:

- Rolled pockets - a tiny strip of tissue is rolled to create a tube. The tube acts as a fitting to accept the spreader. This makes the spreader removeable.

- Internal pockets - a pocket is created to accept the spar. The spar is removeable.

- Folded corners - the corner is folded over the spar and glued. Not removeable.

- Paper patches - a patch of paper is placed over the spar. Glue is used to hold the spar in place. The patches can be functional, decorative or both. Not removeable.

Tip: Whichever method you use to attach the frame to the sail, make sure the finished kite is symmetrical with the left side identical to the right side in flexibility, weight, and area. Setting the angle of flight is described in the following section.

Dihedral techniques

One of the most dramatic improvements that an Eddy kite offered over the previous version of the old diamond kite is the "dihedral" or "v" shape of the frame. This shape adds to the stability of the kite.

Some kites have flexible wings and automatically create the dihedral in flight. Other kites use a fixed frame.

A simple dihedral kite

Kites that use a frame of wood, carbon, or fiberglass may require you to form a fixed dihedral or "curve." The most important issue is that both sides are equal in every respect. The same size, thickness of spars, and dihedral angle.

Choose a method that you like. You'll find that one method may work better than others.

You can build a dihedral into your kite in multiple ways. Here are a few ideas to try:

Folded paper

For kites that are two inches (5 cm) or smaller, just folding the sail may be adequate because the crease adds strength along the fold.

About 150 degrees

Break and re-glue

Setting a proper dihedral

You can build your kite flat, then create the proper angle by cutting the spreader in the middle, lifting the wings an equal amount, and using glue to reset the joint at the new angle. This creates a nice sharp angle, but the joint may be weak.

Soaking and drying

Some woods can be soaked in water for 12 hours, bent, then dried on a jig so they hold the bend. This takes time, but many spreaders can be soaked at the same time. When dry, you can attach the spreader to the sail.

Heat and cool

For bamboo, you can heat it with a candle, then bend it and let it cool. This method gives almost instant results. This method is very popular because you can create many shapes with the bamboo, not just a dihedral.

Tip: To bend, use a candle or a low wattage soldering iron. From 15 to 30 watts works fine.

Straighten or curl

Fishing line works well, but it may still be curled from being stored on a round spool. To remove the curl, wrap it around a long board and bake it for an hour at 300 degrees, then cut it to size. To add curl, wrap it around a can instead of a flat board.

Flexing

Paintbrush bristles and other thin fibers can be used for spreaders too. They start straight, but their advantage is that they bend or "give" in strong wind.

Bracing

This is the brace

Another method is to glue a straight spar to the leading edges that's slightly smaller than the span of the kite. This will give the spreader a V-shape.

Tension lines

Yet another method of forming a dihedral is by putting tension on the spreader to keep it bent. The advantage of this method is that you can release the tension and store the kite flat. This works well for spars made from carbon, fiberglass or bamboo. Here's how to make the tension line:

1. Fold a piece of thread to create the tension line

2. Knot the thread twice to create two loops

3. Put stops on the spreader using glue or a wrap of thread then attach it to the sail

4. Use the loops to bow the spreader

Spreader
Tension line with loops

Both sides do not need loops and stops. Putting a loop on one side works just fine but make sure that the weight is balanced. Wrapping the loop twice (or more) will increase the bow for strong wind.

Bridle techniques

The bridle point is the point where the flying line connects to the kite.

The bridle does two things, it sets the angle of attack into the wind, and it supports the kite at one or more points to give it the strength needed to prevent flexing, flapping and broken spars. Some kites use many bridle points, but most miniature kites use a single bridle point because it's simple and the small sails don't require any additional support. A good starting place is 1/3 of the way down from the top of the kite.

Moving the bridle

The best way to increase the stability of your kite is to find the ideal bridle point. By moving that point higher or lower you change the angle of attack of the kite, so move the bridle only a *tiny* bit then test-fly the kite again.

In general, moving the bridle point *toward the top* of the kite makes the kite fly at a higher angle but also makes it less stable. Think of this as, "riding on top of the wind." (See: bridle point "a")

In general, moving the bridle point *toward the bottom* of the kite makes the kite fly at a lower angle but makes it more stable. Think of this as, "facing the wind." (See: bridle point "b")

The best bridle location may be higher or lower.

Techniques for attaching the bridle

There are many techniques for attaching the bridle to the kite. Some techniques are simpler, while others are stronger, more adjustable, or look prettier. Here are a few:

Bridle technique	Advantages	Example
Glue or tape the bridle to the front of the kite.	This is very simple and easy	
Use a needle to go through the front and attach the line to the back of the kite with tape or glue.	This is a little extra effort, but looks better from the front	
Use a needle to go through the front, then tie the line around the spine and glue it in place. This prevents the bridle from being pulled off.	Looks good and the results are very strong	
Create a keel using a piece of double-stick tape inside a fold. Attach the flying line using glue, tape, or a few holes in the keel. Making holes is the lightest method and allows you to choose the hole that flies best.	Keels add stability	
Consider using an adjustable bridle as seen in the diagram at right. The smaller loop can slide up and down the longer line, but when you tighten the small loop, it locks in place on the thread. This allows you to adjust for the current wind conditions. The knot is called a Prusik knot and it's easy to make by wrapping the loop around the longer line twice.	This method is adjustable and can be readjusted easily	
Another form of an adjustable bridle is a simple loop that slips through two holes in the kite sail. If the holes are small, they'll hold the thread in place, otherwise you'll need a bit of tape. Tugging on the loop adjusts the bridle point up or down.	Adjustable	

Tail techniques

Kite tails add drag to increase the stability of the kite. The tail should be as light as possible and placed at the bottom of the center of the kite. Tails can also be placed in pairs along the bottom edge. They can be split in half, curled, twisted, folded, stretched, tapered, flared, knotted, joined, decorated, striped or have their edges feathered.

Tail material

Mylar tinsel is frequently used by miniature kite builders because it's very inexpensive and can be bought in bulk in a variety of colors. Most party and craft stores sell it. Tissue paper works well and can be cut into strips using pair of scissors, a razor knife or a shredding machine. Mylar cassette tape is plentiful and works very well. People who tie flies for fishing have many choices available to them.

Length of tail

The length of the tail is usually determined by the size of the kite. Try a tail that's about seven times the length of the kite and 1/8" (3 mm) wide. You can make a longer tail by splicing two pieces together. This works but remember that it's easier to cut the tail shorter than to make it longer. Adding tails or increasing the length of an existing tail may improve the flight of your kite.

Tip: If you wish to make tails from a sheet of tissue paper or from a sheet from a garbage bag, here's a shortcut: instead of trying to cut long strips one at a time, roll the sheet into a tight tube, then cut off chunks of the tube. It's much faster and easier.

Attaching tails using tape

1. Place the tail flat on your work surface
2. Using tweezers, lift one of the pieces of tape
3. Place the tape squarely on the tail, halfway off as shown
4. Using tweezers, lift the "tape and tail" then press it onto the kite
5. Make sure the tail is aligned with the kite for best flights

Tip: When attaching tails, consider using double-sided tape. The tape can be completely hidden by the tail giving a very clean look to the finished kite.

Flying lines

You can use just about any thread including nylon, cotton, silk, polyester, spectra, rayon, or even human hair!

Thread for small kites

For most miniature kites, use the cheapest thread you can find. You can get inexpensive thread at any sewing store. Some discount stores sell small spools of thread that are convenient because the spools are so small that you can use one and throw it away when it becomes tangled. The smallest spools only contain 30' (9 meters) of thread, but that's usually plenty for a miniature kite and the package contains 50 colors.

During the manufacturing process, cotton thread is twisted. This causes it to create knots easily. Thread made of nylon, polyester, and silk are continuous filament and are less prone to knots. Thin silk (#100) is more expensive and may be harder to find.

Smaller kites

For smaller and lighter miniature kites use 40 denier nylon. They come on spools so they're easy to handle and they're both very thin and strong. Another alternative is to find unwaxed dental floss and carefully remove a single strand from the floss. Both nylon and floss filaments are good for all but the very lightest miniatures such as film and boron creations.

Smallest kites

For boron and film miniature kites use a single fiber of dental floss or spectra.

Spectra is a fiber invented by NASA that is thin, strong, and has low stretch. This is the lightest thread by far. Spectra fibers are so thin that they are difficult to see and handle. A single fiber has so little weight that it "floats around" making it hard to get back in the box after flying a kite! To use spectra for a tiny kite, find unbraided spectra line and pull out individual strands.

General building tips

- Lightweight kites fly better, so use the lightest materials possible and use very little glue.

- There is usually a tradeoff between weight and strength where the stronger material is usually heavier. That's not always the case so try the lightest material first!

- Pay attention to the grain of the wood. For strength, the grain should go along the wood, lengthwise.

- Always keep your flying line attached to your kite. However, you may wish to detach it from your flying wand. To do this, you can make "tape tabs" by folding a piece of tape over the end of your flying line. The sticky part can be easily attached to a flying rod or antenna while the non-sticky tab will make it easy to pull off.
  Result: It's easy to detach the kite line from the flying wand and put it away.

- "It's all in the details."

- Japanese tissue is very lightweight and has a grain; most domestic tissue papers do not. Tear the tissue in both directions. If it tears straight in one direction but ragged in the other, it's probably pretty good tissue. Gift wrapping tissue is a fair choice. Don't use toilet paper or bathroom tissue for your sails. They sag and rip too easily.

- Apply tiny pieces of tape with a toothpick or tweezers.

- The plastic from unused photo negatives can be cut into strips and used as spreaders.

- Cut many kite sails at once instead of one at a time.

- You can flatten tissue paper by ironing it. Use the "cotton" setting on your iron. Don't linger! You may wish to sandwich the tissue paper between pieces of typing paper. That isn't necessary unless the tissue has ink that might transfer.

- To get two tails or two spars cut to the same length, place them side-by-side and cut them both at the same time.

- Use a small paint brush and model airplane dope to attach two sheets of tissue paper together. Very little overlap is needed to create a good bond.

- Don't use toothpicks for spars, bamboo is a better choice.

- Check the shape of your kite before you fly it. Wings can warp or crease from humidity, heat, handling, or from long periods of storage.

- Use short lines to fly small kites. 12-18 inches (30-45 cm) of thread is usually enough.

- Store your kites in separate boxes to protect them. Clear plastic boxes such as CD jewel boxes, cassette tape boxes, and baseball card boxes make it easy to identify what's inside.

- Keep your keel straight, your spine firm, and remember that lighter kites fly better!

Flying your kite

Some miniature kites will fly at walking speed while others require more wind and can fly outdoors. Some are more stable, some fly slowly, all of them will fly best in smooth air.

One way to fly your miniature kite is by using a flying wand.

Kite must fly above this point ⟶

This can be any stick (a wooden dowel, an old TV antenna, or a collapsible pointer) that's one to four feet long. Attach about 18 inches (45 cm) of thread to your kite, then tape the opposite end of the thread to the end of your flying wand. As you move the flying wand slowly in a circle, the kite will fly. Start slowly. Then, try moving the kite faster. Don't flick your wrist. Use long, steady sweeps of your arm. The kite is not flying until it is above the tow point on where you attached the thread to the stick.

Automated animation

It's a typical misconception that you should use a fan to fly a small kite. Fans generate turbulence, they don't provide smooth air, so don't use them to fly your kite. Wind tunnels are complicated and can be large and expensive.

A solution is to build a kite flying machine such as the one described on page 25 of Harm van Veen's book called, "The Tao of Kiteflying." The machine has a motor that makes a stick sweep a five-foot circle. The kite flies from a thread attached to the end of the stick. If you wish to study flight, the flying machine is ideal because:
- it's portable, and easily stored
- it's inexpensive to build
- the air against the kite is smooth and consistent resulting in superior flight

Increasing kite stability

If you'd like to improve the way a kite flies, there are many ways you can increase the stability of your kite. A simple method is to add more tails. You can also add longer tails, add fins (keels) at the bottom, increase the dihedral, add a drogue, add bridle lines, add vents, reduce the weight, or allow the wings to flex.

Flying line

For kites of all sizes, the weight of the flying line should match to the size and pull of the kite. Miniature kites usually have very little sail area and very little pull so any type of sewing thread will make an acceptable flying line. You can use the cheapest cotton thread, or you can try to find thin nylon, polyester, silk, or rayon thread. Many discount stores offer spools of thread very cheaply. You may want a variety of colors to coordinate the color of the thread with the colors in the kite.

Don't use button thread, dental floss, wool, or yarn. They're too heavy and usually more expensive than sewing thread.

Winders

A winder allows you to store thread on a bobbin, card, or spool so that you can easily release and rewind the thread during flight. Floss cards are available at most craft stores. Winders are best for outdoor flight or very large gymnasiums where you may wish to fly higher.

You can reuse a spool from ribbon or fishing line, or you can build a winder for your thread that imitates the spools used for larger kites:

Winder made from a spool and a dowel. Full size.

Winder made from a sheet of wood. Full size.

Plans for building easy mini kites

Miniature kites are a small part of the kite world. Sorry for the pun.
We can further divide the category of miniature kites into a few branches:

Category	Example
Reproductions	Cody kite
Kid's kites	Butterfly kite
Tiny kites	Tiny heart kite
Ultra-lightweight kites	Cube kite
Outdoor kites	Firecracker kite

There are twenty-six plans below for miniature kites you can build at home. Before you build them, pay close attention to the difficulty and the recommended materials. Build an easy one first such as the "Peartop kite," "Heart kite," "Barn door kite," or "Noodle kite." Later, you may wish to design your own kites.

Peartop kite

Size:	1.5" (4 cm) wide
Difficulty:	Easy
Time to build:	10 minutes

This is a simple kite to build and a great first project. It flies easily at walking speed and will amaze others.

Materials:

- Sail: Wrapping tissue
- Spars: None
- Tail: Mylar tinsel or tissue paper 8" (20 cm) long
- Line: Sewing thread
- Tape: Cellophane tape

Tools:

- Cut: Scissors
- Color: Markers or colored pencils.

Half Template:

Bridle Point

Fold

Method:

1. Fold a piece of tissue paper in half. Keep any decorations on the outside.

2. Cut out the "Half Template" above and align the template with the fold.

3. Draw the <u>outline</u> of the template onto the outside tissue paper once.

4. Mark the circled spot on the tissue paper too. This is the bridle point.

5. Cut out the tissue paper while it is folded.

6. Unfold.

7. Tape a tail to the bottom corner.

8. Tape on the thread at the bridle point in the center.

Bridle Point

9. Look at the top of the kite to make sure it has a slight angle.

Top view:

Front of kite

10. Fly the tiny kite at walking speed.

Heart kite

Size:	1" wide (2.5 cm)
Difficulty:	Easy
Time to build:	15 minutes

This tiny heart kite is small enough to fit inside a matchbox. It's easy to make but it requires very lightweight paper and very thin thread.

Materials: Sail: Thin tissue such as Japanese tissue
Spars: None
Tail: 9" (23 cm) of typical sewing thread
Line: 9" (23 cm) of fine thread such as #100 silk or smaller
Tape: Cellophane tape

Tools: Cut: Scissors
Color: Highlighter or magic markers

Side View

Method:

1. Draw the words onto lightweight tissue paper.

2. Fold the tissue paper in half with the decorations on the outside.

3. While the paper is still folded, cut around the heart making sure to cut cleanly and equally.

4. Unfold the paper.

5. Attach the tail to the bottom, back of the kite at the bottom point. Use a tiny dot of glue or a tiny square of cellophane tape. The actual size is:

6. Attach the flying line at the bridle point: ⊕

7. Fly slowly indoors using a flying wand. The flying wand is very important for a kite this small. Check the paper often to make sure the "top view" is correct without curl.

Template

Fold

HAPPY VALENTINES DAY

Top view:

Front of kite

Barn door kite

Size:	4" (10 cm) wide
Difficulty:	Easy
Time to build:	15 minutes

This kite flies outdoors in light wind with a 4" (10 cm) wingspan. This is a great way to reuse gift wrapping paper.

Materials:
- Sail: Wrapping paper (not tissue)
- Spars: 4" long x 1/4" (10 cm x 6 mm) wide strip from a 2-liter plastic bottle and a plastic coffee stirrer
- Tail: 20" x 1/2" (50 x 12 cm) strip of wrapping paper
- Line: Sewing thread
- Tape: Cellophane tape

Tools:
- Cut: Scissors
- Color: Highlighter or magic markers

Method:

1. Cut out the template on the right.

2. Fold a piece of wrapping paper in half with the decorations on the outside.

3. Trace the outline from the template onto the wrapping paper sail.

4. Cut out the wrapping paper while it is still folded.

5. Cut the coffee stirrer to length and use tape to attach to the center of the back of the sail.

6. Make the spreader 4" (10cm) long and 1/4" (6 mm) wide by cutting the strip of plastic from a 2-liter plastic bottle. The final strip should have a curve in it for dihedral.

Template

Spine

7. Tape on the spreader between the corners.

8. Tape the thread to the front of the kite at the bridle point location "⊕" as seen on the template.

    Bridle Point

9. Tape a 20" (50 cm) tail that's 1/2" (12 mm) wide to the bottom of the back of the kite.

10. Pinch bottom of spine.

    20" long (50 cm)

11. Fly indoors or outdoors!

Guardian Kite

Size:	2 1/2" (6.5 cm) wide
Difficulty:	Easy
Time to build:	15 minutes

This kite is small, has no sticks and flies indoors at walking speed. While preparing for a doodle kite workshop, this kite was created by accident when I bridled a piece of leftover wrapping paper from between the doodle kites! It is unusual because it flies beautifully without a tail. It is therefore origami.

Materials: Sail: Wrapping paper
Spars: None
Tail: Optional
Line: Sewing thread
Tape: Cellophane tape

Tools: Cut: Scissors
Color: Highlighter or magic markers

Template

Bridle Point

Fold

Method:

1. Fold the wrapping paper in half.

2. Cut out the template and use it to trace the shape of the Guardian onto the wrapping paper.

3. Cut out the shape of the Guardian.

4. Unfold the tissue.

5. Tape on the flying line just below the bridle point. ← Bridle Point

6. Fly it well.

Top   Bottom Section   Top

Top View of correct wing angles

Comet kite

Size:	2.5" (6.5 cm) wide
Difficulty:	Easy
Time to build:	15 minutes

This kite looks very cool when it is colored to look like flames.

Materials:
- Sail: Wrapping tissue
- Spars: Paintbrush bristles
- Tail: Mylar tinsel 10" (25 cm) long
- Line: Sewing thread
- Tape: Cellophane tape

Tools:
- Cut: Scissors
- Color: Markers

Method:

1. Fold paper in half with decorations on the outside.

2. Trace half of the comet pattern onto the paper.

3. While the paper is folded, cut out the sail.

4. Attach the paintbrush bristle spine to the back using very tiny dots of glue at the top and bottom.

5. Attach paintbrush bristles to the back. They should not overlap the spine. Use tiny dots of glue at the end of each bristle.

6. Attach mylar tail to the bottom of the back.

7. Attach thread to the front at the ⊕

8. Fly slowly.

Bridle Point

Paintbrush bristles held by dots of glue at each end.

Fold

Butterfly kite

Size:	6" (15 cm) wide
Difficulty:	Easy
Time to build:	15 minutes

This design is based on the Eastern Tiger Swallowtail butterfly and is designed for flying outdoors with a long tail. This kite uses regular typing paper for the sail.

Materials:
- Sail: Typing paper
- Spars: 1/2" (13 mm) x 5" (13 cm) strip from a 2-liter plastic bottle
- Spine: Toothpick or bamboo strip 3.5" (9 cm) long
- Tails: Thin garbage bag strips 20" (50 cm) long
- Line: Sewing thread
- Tape: Cellophane tape

Tools:
- Cut: Scissors
- Color: Highlighter or magic markers

Method:

1. Cut out the page with the butterfly template below.

2. Decorate using a highlighter and/or magic markers.

3. Fold the butterfly in half along the black line in the center of the butterfly.

4. Cut out the butterfly while it is still folded. This will maintain the symmetry.

5. Glue the toothpick in the center of the back behind the black line. This is the spine. Use very little glue. <u>Note</u>: The toothpick is optional.

6. Cut out a plastic strip from a 2-liter bottle. Since a flat butterfly kite doesn't fly well, a curved piece of plastic works best. If you have a flat piece of plastic, bend it in the middle.

7. Position the plastic strip on the back of the kite so that it is horizontal across the back of the butterfly, one inch (2.5 cm) from the top, and centered left and right.

8. Tape on the plastic strip using 3 small pieces of cellophane tape on the left, right, and center. The butterfly should now be curved with wingtips up.

Back view with tails, plastic strip, and wing tips up.

9. Tape the two pairs of tails below the spine on the back of the butterfly at the bottom in the center. Use small pieces of tape. When you're done there should be four tails 20" (50 cm) long.

10. Turn the kite over. Use tape to attach the thread so it meets the front exactly at the "x" mark on the front of your butterfly. The thread is your flying line.

11. Look at the top of the kite and make sure it has the proper "v" shape just like this:

Top view:

Front of kite

12. Enjoy flying your butterfly!

This is the full-size sail. Decorate it first, then fold in half and cut out the butterfly.

Butterfly Template

Mini Bird kite

Size:	3" (8 cm)
Difficulty:	Easy
Time to build:	10 minutes

We built 100 of these kites at an after-dinner workshop in Florida. It didn't take long. With only one spar, my kite design is easy to build and flies outdoors in a light breeze.

Materials:
- Sail: Tissue paper
- Spars: 1 Glass spar 4" (10 cm) long on tape with backing
- Spine: None
- Tails: (2) Strips 20" (50 cm) long – silver sparkle
- Line: 18" (45 cm) Sewing thread
- Tape: (2) Tiny pieces of tape

Tools:
- Cut: Scissors
- Mark: Pencil

Method:

1. Fold the tissue in half:

2. Cut out the Half Template.

3. Align the template with the fold in the tissue:

4. Draw the outline onto the tissue and mark the bridle point location

5. Cut out the tissue and unfold it.

6. Tape the spreader in the center of the back between the wingtips.

7. Bend at the center until you snap the spreader.

40

8. Tape both tails onto the back, at the very bottom, in the center:

   Back

9. Turn over to see the front:

   Front

10. Tape the thread onto the <u>front</u> in the center just below the bridle point with thread above it.

11. Enjoy flying!

Leaf kite

Size:	3" (7.5 cm) wide
Difficulty:	Easy
Time to build:	20 minutes

As you walk down the hall, this kite will fly beside you. When you stop walking this kite will flutter to the ground, just like a leaf.

Materials: Sail: Very lightweight tissue
Spars: Paintbrush bristles
Tail: Tinsel or tissue 1/16" (1.5 mm) wide, and 10" (25 cm) long
Line: Sewing thread
Tape: Glue

Tools: Cut: Scissors
Color: Markers

Method:

1. Fold a piece of tissue paper in half.
2. Cut out this pattern and trace it onto the tissue.
3. Cut the tissue to size.
4. Glue the spine on the back at the fold.
5. Glue 3 horizontal paintbrush bristles.
6. Attach tail at the bottom in the center.
7. Attach thread at tow point.
8. Fly well.

Bridle point

Spine

Template

Sled kite

Size:	6" wide (15 cm)
Difficulty:	Easy
Time to build:	10 minutes

This kite is easy to build because there's no spars, and it's interesting to fly because it can fly without a tail. It flies well indoors, and it will also fly outdoors in a gentle breeze.

Materials:

- Sail: Wrapping tissue
- Spars: None
- Tail: None
- Line: Bridle 16" (40 cm) of thread, sewing thread spool
- Tape: Mylar tape

Tools:

- Cut: Scissors
- Color: Markers
- Ruler: Any straight edge

Method:

1. Cut out the full-size Sled Kite Template below:

Sled Kite Template (Full size)

16" (40 cm) bridle

← Knot here

↑ Center of bridle

2. Place the template over the tissue paper and draw the outline:

3. Cut out the tissue paper but do not crease the center.

4. Fold the sail along dotted lines to give the angle shown:

   Top View

   Front

5. Tape the thread to the corners of both wing tips:

6. After the thread is attached on both sides, mark the <u>exact</u> center of bridle thread and make a loop approximately 1" (2 cm), then tie a knot as shown.

   ← Knot here

   Center of bridle

7. Attach flying line to the loop.

8. Enjoy flying your sled kite indoors and outdoors!

Penguin kite

Size:	4" (10 cm)
Difficulty:	Easy
Time to build:	15 minutes

This kite was inspired by Robert Trepanier who is an amazing kite builder in Montreal. This kite will fly indoors while you walk. The lightweight nature of the kite helps it fly well but the real trick is the overlap of paper on the leading edge.

Materials:

    Sail: Tissue Paper
    Spar: None
    Spine: None
    Tail: (4) Mylar tinsel 12" (30 cm) long
    Line: Sewing thread 18" (45 cm) long
    Tape: (2) tiny bits of tape

Tools: Cut: Scissors
    Color: Markers

Method:

1. Cut out the half-template below.

2. Fold the tissue paper in half.

3. Align the template with the fold in the tissue.

4. Cut out.

5. Unfold and decorate the penguin.

6. Starting at the top, cut a 1" (2.5 cm) slot along the fold.

Cut here.

7. Tape the end of the thread onto the back and push the thread through the slot to the front.

Back

8. Overlap the slot and tape it closed with a tiny bit of tape.

Back

9. Use tiny bits of tape to attach a 12" (30 cm) loop tail. One end to the left toe and the other end to the right toe of the penguin.

10. Fly indoors at walking speed.

Bridle point

Half Template

Tail

Doodle kite

Size:	6.5" (16 cm)
Difficulty:	Easy
Time to build:	15 minutes

This kite flies indoors while you walk. The lightweight nature of the kite helps it fly well. This kite is made to "flex" when it flies adding to the stability of the kite. This kite was created for a workshop at the festival called, "Kites on Ice" in Madison, Wisconsin.

Materials:

    Sail: Tissue Paper
    Spar: (1) 10-pound fishing line
    Spine: (1) Brush bristle
    Tail: (4) Mylar tinsel 12" (30 cm) long
    Line: Sewing thread 18" (45 cm) long
    Tape: (8) tape bits

Tools: Cut: Scissors, Tweezers
          Color: Markers

Method:

1. Fold the tissue paper in half.

2. Cut out the half-template.

Bridle point

Half-Template

The fold goes here.

3. Place the template over the tissue paper.

4. Align the template with the fold and draw the outline.

5. Mark the bridle point then cut out the sail:

6. Unfold the sail.

7. Decorate the sail with doodles using pens, pencils or markers, not crayons or paint.

8. Lay the kite face down.

9. Cut the spine to size.

10. Attach the spine to the center <u>on the back</u> using two pieces of tape:

11. Use two pieces of tape to attach the spreader straight across to the left and right corners.

12. Place a third piece of tape in the center.

13. Trim off any extra spreader or tape.

49

14. Tape <u>all four tails</u> to the bottom center of the back, using one or more pieces of tape.

Tails

15. Turn the kite face up.

16. With the spars and tails on the back, tape the thread to the <u>front</u> of the kite. The thread should meet the kite at the bridle point. <u>Notice</u>: the thread is above the tape.

Correct: Incorrect:

17. Enjoy flying your kite indoors while you walk!

Chopstick kite

Size:	1.5" (38 mm) wide
Difficulty:	Easy
Time to build:	10 minutes

This kite is both simple and unusual. You need very few materials to build it, but the sail needs a little bit of stiffness to it so that it will fly without spars. The crease down the center is very important and must be straight because it does two things at the same time: it adds stiffness to give the kite shape and provides a dihedral so it can fly. This doesn't fly as well as others.

Materials:
- Sail: Gift wrap or wrapping tissue
- Spars: None
- Tail: Optional
- Line: Sewing thread 18" (45 cm) long
- Tape: Cellophane tape

Tools:
- Cut: Scissors, Tweezers

Template

Fold

Method:

1. Fold sail in half with decoration on the outside.

2. Cut out the sail.

3. Cut a small piece of tape as shown.

4. Tape the thread onto the kite at the place shown with a piece of tape this big:

5. Set the angle for the kite:

   Correct angle for fold

6. Make sure the kite is straight and symmetrical from top to bottom.

7. Fly slowly indoors.

Noodle kite

Size:	3" (7 cm) wide
Difficulty:	Easy
Time to build:	10 minutes

This small version of a noodle kite makes a great bookmark! The original kite was 11 feet (3.5 meters) tall and 30 inches (75 cm) wide and twisted like a noodle in flight! This one will fly at walking speed indoors. Designed by David Ellis and based on the Chopstick kite.

Materials:
- Sail: Wrapping tissue
- Spars: None – the fold on the center line adds stiffness
- Tail: None
- Line: Sewing thread
- Tape: Cellophane

Tools:
- Cut: Scissors
- Color: Many wrapping tissue papers are already decorated. If you have plain wrapping paper decorate with markers.

Method:

1. Fold the tissue paper in half.
2. Cut a 1" (2.5 cm) wide strip of folded tissue that's 8" (20 cm) long.
3. Cut ends at an angle to form points shown.
4. Unfold to be 2" (5 cm) wide.
5. Decorate.
6. Attach flying line at a point one inch (2.5 cm) from the top.
7. Crease the bottom half of the kite. That's why the kite in the photo looks tapered. There's more fold at the bottom.
8. Fly at a moderate walking speed.

Korean fighter kite

Size:	2" (5 cm) wide
Difficulty:	Easy
Time to build:	20 minutes

The kite is a steady flyer indoors.

Materials:
- Sail: Lightweight tissue
- Spars: Brush bristle
- Tails: Two strips of tissue 12" (30 cm) long
- Line: Any thread
- Tape: Cellophane

Tools:
- Cut: Scissors
- Color: Colored tissue and markers

Method:

1. Fold the tissue paper in half.
2. Mark the tissue according to the template below.
3. Cut out the rectangle.
4. Optional: Cut out the center circle or just draw it.
5. Unfold the tissue.
6. Optional: Turn to the back and use bits of tape to attach brush bristle from corner to corner.
7. Attach the tails at the bottom corners with bits of tape.
8. Attach flying line so it meets the kite at the bridle point.
9. Fly at a moderate walking speed.

Template

Bridle point

Fold

53

Rokkaku kite

Size:	3.5" wide (8 cm)
Difficulty:	Easy
Time to build:	10 minutes

The Rokkaku kite is a Japanese style that's shortened to "Rok" (pronounced "rock.") This kite is so small we should call it a pebble. The Rokkaku kite is a steady flyer.

Materials:

- Sail: Lightweight tissue 3" (8 cm) wide
- Spars: broom bristle for the spine
  2 spreaders of 8# fishing line
- Tail: (3) 12" (30 cm) mylar tails
- Line: Thread
- Tape: (10) pieces

Tools:
- Cut: Scissors
- Draw: Pencil or pen

Bridle Point

Half Template

Fold

Method:

1. Fold tissue in half with decorations on the outside:

2. Cut out the "Half Template."

3. Match the long edge to the fold in the tissue paper.

54

4. Draw the outline and mark the bridle point on the tissue exactly where you see it on the half template:

5. Cut out the shape while the tissue paper is still folded:

6. Unfold the tissue:

7. Place the sail face down on the table to see the back.

8. Tape the vertical spine onto the back:

9. Tape the horizontal spreaders to the back:

10. Trim off any excess spine or spreader.

11. Tape all three tails to the center of the bottom.

12. Turn the kite over to see the front.

13. Tape thread at the very center of the bridle point shown by the circle on the half template.

14. Give a slight fold to the kite to give it a "v" shape like this:

    Top view: Front of kite

15. Fly the kite at walking speed. If it swims left and right, crease the center a bit more.

56

Ghost kite

Size:	3" (8 cm) wide
Difficulty:	Easy
Time to build:	10 minutes

The ghost kite made from a simple paper fold.

Materials: Sail: Lightweight tissue
Spars: Thin but stiff bamboo spine and thin, flexible spreaders
Tail: 10" (25 cm) mylar tail
Line: Any thread
Tape: Tape

Tools: Cut: Scissors
Color: Colored tissue

Method:

1. Fold tissue in half.
2. Use the template to cut to shape. Notice that the template does not use independent arms because that will cause the tissue paper to curl.
3. Draw in the eyes and mouth using black markers.
4. Attach a tail to the bottom center.
5. Attach flying line at bridle point shown.
6. Fly at a slow walking speed.

Template

Bridle Point

Fold

57

Train of kites

Size:	1.5" (4 cm) wide
Difficulty:	Easy
Time to build:	30 minutes

These three pear-top kites form a kite train and fly as a single kite. They're very charming in flight and multiple trains can be attached together to form long chains of fun. A train of three kites is described here because it is easier to manage in flight.

Materials:

- Sail: Mylar gift wrap
- Spars: None
- Tail: Mylar tinsel 8" (20 cm) long
- Line: Spool of thread
- Tape: Cellophane tape, glue, or cement

Tools:

- Cut: Scissors, needle, tweezers
- Color: Markers or colored pencils.

Half Template — Bridle Point

Fold

Method:

1. Take three pieces of tissue paper.

2. Lay them on top of each other and fold them in half together. Keep them as close together as possible.

3. Cut out the "Half Template" above.

4. Align the template with the fold.

5. Draw the outline of the template onto the outside tissue paper once. Mark the bridle point on the tissue paper too.

6. Cut out all three sails at the same time so they are identical in size.

7. Unfold.

8. Tape a tail to each bottom corner of each sail:

9. Pass the needle through all three kites at the bridle point shown as a circle on the template.

10. Glue the end of the thread to the back of the last kite.

11. Move them 8 inches (20 cm) apart.

8"

8"

To spool of thread

12. Use a tiny dot of glue to attach each sail to the thread. Be sure the thread is perpendicular to the kite before it dries.

Dot of glue

Back of kite

13. Looking at the top of each kite to make sure <u>each kite</u> has a slight angle.

Top view:

Front of kite

14. Fly the train at walking speed.

Plans for moderate and challenging kites

If you have built a few kites before and have excellent model-building skills, you might want to try something more challenging. Pick a plan from the ones below. There are a variety of styles to choose from including kites that fly indoors and/or outdoors.

Six friends kite

Size:	4" (10 cm) wide
Difficulty:	Moderate
Time to build:	15 minutes

These kites are friends and they fly closely together because they're attached at the hip. This kite is one of my own designs.

Materials:
- Sail: Thin tissue such as Japanese tissue
- Spars: Paintbrush bristles for all spars
- Tails: Five tails of 12" (30 cm) long mylar tinsel
- Line: Sewing thread
- Tape: Cellophane tape

Tools:
- Cut: Scissors
- Color: Highlighter or magic markers, ruler

Method:

1. Cut out the template at right.

2. Fold a piece of tissue paper in half. If the paper has decorations, keep them on the outside.

3. While the paper is still folded use the template to cut the sail.

4. Unfold the paper.

5. Use a ruler to draw the grid lines on the paper in black. Color some of the diamonds using highlighters or magic markers.

6. On the back, attach five vertical paint brush bristles at the locations shown below.

7. Attach the horizontal spreader. Two overlapping bristles may be needed to match the width. If you use two, make sure they are identical in length and each starts in the outer corners.

8. Attach six tails to the back of the kite at the points shown. Use a tiny dot of glue or a tiny square of cellophane tape this big:

9. Attach the flying line at the bridle point: ⊕

10. Fly slowly indoors.

62

Single cell box kite

Size:	4" (10 cm) wide
Difficulty:	Moderate
Time to build:	30 minutes

To fly well, it's important to make this kite square all around.

Materials: Sail: Thin tissue such as Japanese tissue
Spars: Balsa wood about 1/20" (1.3 mm) square
Tail: 9" (22 cm) of typical sewing thread
Line: 9" (22 cm) of thread
Tape: Cellophane tape

Tools: Cut: Razor blade, sandpaper
Color: Highlighter or magic markers

Build Frame

1. <u>Cut:</u> 12 balsa sticks that are 4 inches (10 cm) long. Use balsa wood. Toothpicks are too heavy. Sand until exactly equal.

2. <u>Build bottom square:</u> On a flat surface, apply *very little* glue to attach four sticks. This creates a square about 4" (10 cm) on each side.

3. <u>Top square:</u> Build an identical square for the top.

4. <u>Attach connectors:</u> Glue four "connector" sticks to the bottom, one in each corner. To get them pointing straight up, you may prop them up against a book until the glue has dried. Doing this step right will make the next step easier.

5. <u>Lay the top on the connectors:</u> Put a tiny dot of glue on the ends of the four connectors and carefully attach top.

Cover

6. While the glue on the frame is drying, decorate the 4" x 17" (10 cm x 43 cm) paper with markers.

7. Glue (or dope) the tissue to the frame. Glue one edge at a time leaving the top and bottom open. Use tiny dots of glue to wrap tissue around the frame one side at a time.

8. Trim off excess paper with a razor blade or scissors. Be very careful!

Attach Bridle

9. Attach the flying line 1/8" (3 mm) from the top using a needle and thread to tie a knot around the stick.

10. To prevent the bridle from slipping up or down, put a tiny dab of glue between the thread and the stick.

Fly

11. Fly indoors using thread. To avoid breakage, don't touch the kite with your hands.

Genki kite

Size:	6" (15 cm) wide
Difficulty:	Moderate
Time to build:	15 minutes

This kite is one of my own designs. I really like the sleek shape. With polyester fabric and carbon fibers, this kite is strong enough to fly outdoors in light wind.

Materials:
- Sail: 0.5-ounce polyester fabric
- Spars: Micro-carbon 0.02" diameter
- Tails: Three, 18" (45 cm) long, ½" (18 mm) wide polyester fabric or similar material
- Line: Any thread
- Glue: Cyanoacrylate such as "Crazy Glue"

Tools:
- Cut: Scissors
- Color: Magic markers

Method:

1. Cut out the template.
2. Fold the sail's fabric in half.
3. Draw the outline onto the fabric.
4. Cut out the sail.
5. Draw the graphic onto the fabric.
6. Attach vertical and horizontal spars to the back.
7. Attach three tails that are 18" (45 cm) long to the bottom center.
8. Use a needle to thread the bridle line through the bridle point ⊕ shown on the template.
9. Fly outdoors!

Bridle Point

Template
(Full size)

UFO kite

Size:	4" (10 cm) wide
Difficulty:	Moderate
Time to build:	15 minutes

This kite is one of my own designs. It looks best with a spaceman or alien inside.

Materials: Sail: Thin tissue such as Japanese tissue
Spars: Paint brush bristles
Tail: Tissue paper in the shape of flames
Line: 18" (45 cm) of thread
Tape: Cellophane tape

Tools: Cut: Scissors
Color: Highlighter or magic markers

Method:

1. Cut out the template.

2. Fold tissue in half.

3. Place the template over the tissue with the long edge at the crease in the tissue.

4. Draw the outline onto the tissue.

5. Cut out the sail.

6. Color the tails in red and yellow and add other details with pens and markers.

7. Attach paint brush bristle spars to stiffen the paper horizontally and vertically.

8. Attach thread at the bridle point ⊕ on the template.

9. Fly! To improve the flight, extend the center tail.

Roller kite

Size:	4" (10 cm) wide
Difficulty:	Moderate
Time to build:	30 minutes

The name "Roller" comes from the German "Rolloplan" and has nothing to do with flipping or rolling. This dual-sail kite is a steady flyer in light wind.

Materials: Sail: Thin tissue such as Japanese tissue
Spars: Bamboo or carbon, paintbrush bristles
Tail: None
Line: 9" (23 cm) of thread
Tape: Cellophane tape

Tools: Cut: Scissors
Color: Highlighter or magic markers

Method:

1. Cut out the template in two parts, top and bottom.
2. Decorate the sail or use wrapping tissue that is already decorated.
3. Fold in half.
4. Use the template to cut out the tissue paper.
5. The spine should be bamboo or carbon while the vertical sides should be connected using paintbrush bristles.
6. Attach thread at the bridle point ⊕ shown on the template.
7. Fly!

66

Firecracker kite

Size:	4" (10 cm) wide
Difficulty:	Moderate
Time to build:	15 minutes

This is a small version of a noodle kite. My original was 7 inches (18 cm) tall and the first copy was 7 feet (2.1 m) tall. This curved miniature kite will fly outdoors in gentle breezes.

Materials:
- Sail: Tyvek is available from the post office in the form of mailing envelopes. Cut a piece of Tyvek 7" x 4" (18 x 10 cm)
- Spars: Curved strips from a plastic soda bottle are used for stiffness and to give dihedral. 4" (10 cm) x 1/4" (6 mm)
- Tail: Black yarn with red mylar strips at the bottom 36" (90 cm) long
- Line: Sewing thread
- Tape: Cellophane

Tools:
- Cut: Scissors, razor blade or razor knife
- Color: Magic markers, highlighter or multiple colors of tissue glued together.

Method:

1. Decorate the Tyvek paper with red stripes using markers.
2. Draw the fuse on the sail with a black magic marker.
3. Attach the tail at the bottom of the fuse so it looks like one continuous piece.
4. Cut the Tyvek to size and be sure to make the top and bottom rounded and the sides exactly equal.
5. Attach three plastic strips as spreaders. This will set the curve of the sail. See the Barn Door kite for details.
6. Attach bridle. A two-point adjustable bridle is recommended.

Bridle setting

Hawk kite

Size:	6" (15 cm) wide
Difficulty:	Moderate
Time to build:	20 minutes

The hawk kite is a popular bird and looks great in black with a white face and black eyes.

Materials:
- Sail: Lightweight tissue
- Spars: Thin but stiff bamboo spine and thin, flexible brush bristles for battens
- Tail: 12" (30 cm) mylar tail
- Line: Any thread
- Tape: Cement

Tools:
- Cut: Razor blade
- Color: Colored tissue

Method:

1. Fold black or dark grey tissue in half.
2. Cut to shape.
3. Color the head white or glue white tissue on top.
4. Draw in the eyes using black markers.
5. Attach spine.
6. Attach spreader.
7. Attach battens directly onto the sail.
8. Attach tail.
9. Attach flying line at bridle point shown.
10. Fly at a slow walking speed.

Bridle Point

Template

Fold

Battens

68

Sparrow kite

Size:	4" (10 cm wide)
Difficulty:	Advanced
Time to build:	45 minutes

This miniature kite was inspired by the Cody.

Materials:
- Sail: Tissue paper
- Spars: Bamboo skewer
- Tail: Approximately 16" (40 cm) wool or 24" (60 cm) audio cassette tape for the tail
- Line: Sewing thread
- Tape: None
- Glue: Wood glue and a glue stick

Tools:
- Cut: Scissors, craft knife, and cutting board. Heavy card (for templates)
- Color: Markers
- Holes: Sewing needle (any size)

Making spars for the Sparrow

The bamboo skewer can be split, shaved, sanded and trimmed into very thin spars. You will need three spars 4" (10 cm) long, and two spars 2" (5 cm) long.

Making sails

You need two templates, of the following dimensions:

The edge marked with the dotted line should be placed on the crease of your folded tissue, so that when they are cut out, you end up with diamond-shaped pieces of tissue. You need one of the longer pieces, and three of the smaller pieces. Pierce a small hole in the center of the larger piece and one of the smaller pieces.

Sails

Spars

Construction

1. Lay one 10cm spar over the two pierced sails as shown. Leave a gap of 2.5cm between, and 2.5cm of the spar projecting beyond the smaller sail. Glue the spar to the sails using the glue stick.

2. Using the glue stick again, glue 7.5cm of another 10cm spar. Insert the **_unglued_** part of the spar through the hole in the larger sail, under the central spar.

3. Lay the spar down on the sail, and carefully press it in place. Repeat this with the final 10cm spar, on the other side of the larger sail.

4. Repeat a similar process with the smaller sail, gluing 2.5cm of the 5cm spars.

5. The kite should now have each sail firmly glued to a spar, with the lower ends of the spars forming four leg-like projections from the bottom of the kite. Turn the kite over, so that it lies flat, with the "legs" uppermost.

6. Take two pieces of scrap plastic bag and slide them under a pair of legs. Only the spars and a thin line of sail (along the crease) should be exposed.

7. Place one of the remaining sail pieces across the glued spars. Press it down firmly.

8. Repeat with the other pair of legs & the remaining sail piece, then carefully open the spars into an uneven 'X' and remove the scraps of plastic.

9. Using the needle, sew a small loop of thread around the crossing-point of the larger wing spars, and through the smaller sail below. This is where you will attach the bridle. See the illustration below.

10. Carefully prop the sails in the 'X' shape, with the longer sails uppermost. Apply a drop of wood glue to the crossing point of the front & rear wing spars. *Allow the glue to dry fully before going any further*.

11. Attach the tail with glue or a small piece of tape.

12. Attach a flying line (more sewing thread) to the loop of thread.

13. Get out in the wind!

Cody kite

Size:	10" (25cm) wide
Difficulty:	Advanced
Time to build:	3 hours

This kite takes longer to build but it is a steady flyer indoors.

Materials:
- Sail: Japanese tissue
- Spars: Balsa 1/20" (1.25 mm) square
- Tail: None
- Line: Any thread
- Tape: Cement and Dope

Tools:
- Cut: Razor blade
- Color: Colored tissue

Method:

See the detailed plan and directions below.

Balsa Sticks

4
2
6

Balsa Connectors

6

Tissue Paper Verticals

2

2 Balsa Gussets

30 degree cut

Bridle Line
16"

Front

Back

Extended Wing Cody Plan
Ultralightweight Indoor Version
(c) Glenn Davison 1999

Background

The Cody Box kite is a traditional style of kite invented by Samuel Franklin Cody in 1901. Box kites were used to study "fixed wing flight" and led to the creation of the first successful airplane. The Cody design has been adapted to a small-scale using model airplane construction techniques. This kite has a 10-inch (25 cm) wingspan and is made using balsa wood and tissue paper. If you use very little glue, and keep it lightweight and balanced, it will fly indoors at walking speed.

Step 1 - Check your tools and materials

- Clear cement is recommended (or glue).
- Use as little glue as possible. Use a toothpick to dab the glue in place.
- Flat piece of cardboard 9" x 12" (25 x 30 cm) to support the plan
- Clear plastic wrap to protect the plan from glue.
- Razor blade
- Nail file
- Toothpick to apply glue and punch holes
- Balsa sticks, and balsa wood for gussets
- Tissue paper
- Thread for bridle
- Thread for flying line
- The razor blade is very sharp. Don't slice your fingers!
- Balsa is delicate and breaks easily, so will your kite. Handle it as little as possible.

Overview

- ☐ You will build a FRONT and BACK framework and cover them in tissue paper, then you will attach the two layers together with connectors.
- ☐ Check off each step as you go.

Step 2 - Surface Preparation

- ☐ Tape the plan to the cardboard.
- ☐ Tape the plastic wrap over the plan to protect it.
- ☐ Tape one piece of tissue over the plastic wrap with the shiny side of the tissue facing down. This will be the sail for the BACK in the next step.

Step 3 - Cutting the first balsa sticks

We will begin by building the BACK extended wing structure using balsa.
The BACK looks like this:

☐ Cut 2 long verticals.
☐ Cut 2 medium verticals.
☐ Cut 4 short verticals.

Step 4 - Glue sticks to tissue

☐ One at a time, use the toothpick to dot a stick with glue, then quickly attach a stick to the tissue. Use as little glue as possible. Three dots are enough. Do not spread glue on the whole stick.

Step 5 - Glue horizontals onto sticks

☐ Cut the two horizontals.
☐ Glue horizontals on top by dotting the sticks with glue.

Step 6 - Trim the tissue

☐ Trim the box from the center with the razor.
☐ Trim along the outside dotted lines.
☐ The BACK is done. Carefully lift it from the plan.
☐ Attach the wingtip tissue to the wood with a single dot of glue.
☐ Check your work. If any tissue falls away from the sticks, glue it with a small dot.

Step 7 - Clean the building surface

☐ To build the FRONT we'll need a clean building surface. If necessary, repeat step 2 to make sure the building surface is ready. Use the second sheet of tissue paper now.

Step 8 - Build the FRONT

- [ ] Cut and glue 2 long verticals on the sides.
- [ ] Cut and glue 2 short verticals on the center.
- [ ] Cut and glue 2 horizontals on top of verticals as Step 5.
- [ ] Trim box from center of tissue.
- [ ] Trim tissue around the outside on dotted lines.
- [ ] FRONT is done. Carefully lift it from the plan.
- [ ] If they're not attached yet, glue the wingtip tissue to horizontals with a single dot of glue.

Step 9 - Attach the connectors to the BACK

Note: When you attach them, both FRONT and BACK face in the same direction. The tissue acts as "the sail" that will face toward you in flight.
- [ ] Cut 6 short balsa connectors.
- [ ] Equalize their length by sanding them.
- [ ] Use the toothpick to make 6 holes through the BACK tissue at the X marks.
- [ ] Lay the BACK with the tissue side up.
- [ ] Glue the 6 connectors into the holes. They should only extend 1/16" (1.5mm).

These are connectors. Put glue here.

Step 10 - Attach the 6 connectors to the FRONT

- [ ] Put glue on the tips of all 6 of the connectors.
- [ ] Carefully lay the FRONT onto the connectors.

Cut and re-glue wood here, then glue gussets on top of wood.

Step 11 - Add the dihedral angle to the wings

- [ ] Cut or crack the wings where they join the body.
- [ ] Elevate the wingtips to 3 ¼" (8.2 cm) high using paper cups.
- [ ] Re-glue wings to form the dihedral angle. Use very little glue. Make sure the wings are not twisted.
- [ ] Cut out and sand two identical triangular balsa gussets. (See the full-size plan)
- [ ] Glue the gussets over the wing joints to add strength.

Step 12 - Attach tissue paper verticals
- [ ] Cut out a tissue square. It should be long enough to reach between the two verticals on the left side.
- [ ] Attach it to the two vertical sticks on the left. Keep it as flat as possible.
- [ ] Cut out a second tissue square. Attach it to the two vertical sticks on the right.

Step 13 - Add the bridle   Bridle point →

☐ Cut a 16" (40 cm) length of thread.
☐ Attach the ends of the thread to the tops of the sticks
   on the FRONT. (See the full-size plan)
☐ Find the center by hanging the kite from the bridle until it is level, then tie a knot to leave a loop in
   the middle of the bridle. Attach the flying line to the loop.

Step 14 - Fly

☐ Fly your kite gently indoors with long, smooth arm motions! Walking flies best. Don't run.

Building Variations

Many variations are possible. Remember: Additional details may look great, but they may add weight
and cause the kite to fly poorly! Possibilities include:

- Attach tissue strips as tails.   Add centers that divide the boxes in two
- Add a top sail!   Add additional structural balsa strips.
- Add additional bridle lines.   Use multiple colors of tissue
- Add tissue sides to the front.   Attach tissue "decals" such as: stars, stripes

Design your own kite

Size:	Your choice
Difficulty:	Your choice
Time to build:	It's up to you!

Challenge yourself and others to design and build a kite that flies well. This has also been called, "junkyard wars." You can make this challenge into a competition where you supply the materials and the first person to get a kite to fly wins a prize. The kite must fly continuously for 10 seconds above the tow point.

Materials:
- Sail: Tissue paper or wrapping paper
- Spars: Broom bristles, brush bristles, fishing line, or a strip of plastic
- Tail: Wrapping paper or mylar tinsel
- Line: Sewing thread
- Tape: Cellophane tape

Tools:
- Cut: Scissors
- Color: Highlighter or magic markers

Tips for building:

- Draw a sketch of your idea
- Consider starting with a folded piece of tissue paper
- Consider making a template
- Compare your available materials to find the lightest
- Add additional tails to improve flight
- Use the section below to improve the flight of your kite

Improving the flight of your kite

Be careful with your construction and repairs because small mistakes can make a big difference in how well your kite flies. Once it's built, small changes may help to improve the flight of your single line kite. Here's a troubleshooting guide:

Check the tail:
- ☐ Is the tail long enough? Adding tails or lengthening the tail is an easy solution to many problems. Depending on the style of kite, you may need a tail that's seven times the length of your kite or more.
- ☐ Are the tails centered at the bottom of the kite or equally placed on the sides?

Check the bridle point:
- ☐ Is the bridle point to the left, to the right? It should be exactly in the center.
- ☐ Moving the bridle point higher or lower may dramatically improve the flight of your kite. Move it a tiny bit at a time.

Check the sail:
- ☐ The sail should be flat not curled. Flatten the sail by rubbing the back with your fingernail or attach a batten (a small spar on the sail)
- ☐ Is the sail torn or improperly attached to the frame?
- ☐ Is the left side the same size as the right side?

Check the frame:
- ☐ Is the kite too flat? Many kites will fly better when you give them a slight "v" shape. Often, this change will make a big improvement in the flight of the kite.
- ☐ Are there bent or broken sticks?
- ☐ Is the frame straight and symmetrical?
- ☐ Are the spars too heavy? This is a typical problem for new builders. Toothpicks, for example, are far too heavy for most miniature kites. Bamboo can be split.
- ☐ Does the spreader flex equally on the left and right?
- ☐ Does the spine flex too much? If so, you'll see a flapping or pitching motion.

List of websites

Miniature Kites	http://miniatures.kitingusa.com
Galleries	Http://miniatures.kitingusa.com/mini_galleries.htm
Materials	http://miniatures.kitingusa.com/mini_materials.htm
Plans	http://miniatures.kitingusa.com/mini_plans.htm
Tips	http://miniatures.kitingusa.com/mini_tips.htm
Rules for Success	http://miniatures.kitingusa.com/mini_tips_sotich.htm
Contest Results	http://miniatures.kitingusa.com/mini_contest.htm
Vendors & Associations	http://miniatures.kitingusa.com/mini_links.htm
AKA	http://www.kite.org

Bibliography

- The Tao of Kiteflying, The Dynamics of Tethered Flight by Harm van Veen

- Japanese Kites, Concepts and Construction, by Dan Kurahashi. See Chapter 7 for an explanation about how to split bamboo and how to make a Canada Goose, Hummingbird, Pteranodon, butterflies, birds, mini Edo, Coyne, Winged Box and Mini Cody kites. See the weights of different materials on page 4-4.

- Kiteworks by Maxwell Eden. See Chapter 42. Instructions for Eddy, Delta, Optical Confusion and modified Japanese Wan Wan kites.

- Kites in the Classroom by Glenn Davison from the American Kitefliers Association.

- How to Fly a Kite by Glenn Davison from the American Kitefliers Association.

- Kite Workshop Handbook by Glenn Davison from www.amazon.com books.

- Indoor Kiteflying by Glenn Davison from www.amazon.com books.

- Building Free and Recycled Kites by Glenn Davison from www.amazon.com books.

- Kite Physics by Glenn Davison from www.amazon.com books.

Printed in Poland
by Amazon Fulfillment
Poland Sp. z o.o., Wrocław